HE WHO FLIES BY NIGHT

the story of GREY OWL

WRITTEN BY LORI PUNSHON

ILLUSTRATED BY MIKE KEEPNESS

DEDICATIONS

To my children Sarah and Jeff: thank you for our precious story times. You sparked a dream in me and unknowingly continued to nurture it. I also dedicate this book to my husband, Kevin. Thank you for never doubting I could make it happen. Your incredible enthusiasm for this book encouraged me more than you'll ever know. And, of course, thank you for telling me about Grey Owl.

To Mike Keepness: thank you for bringing my words to life through your beautiful artwork. You're an amazing talent and such a joy to work with—I wish you great success in your art career. To Heather Nickel: thank you for embracing my project right from the start. You have been a delight to work with and your expertise has been instrumental in making my dream come true.

LORI PUNSHON

I dedicate the artwork of this book to my beautiful daughter, Rachel Diane Rose. You bring me such happiness every day.
Thank you to my father, Darwin, who has been a constant source of inspiration and encouragement from the very beginning of my art career.

MIKE KEEPNESS

He Who Flies By Night: The Story of Grey Owl

© 2006 Lori Punshon

Punshon, Lori, 1963-

   He who flies by night : the story of Grey Owl / written by Lori Punshon ; illustrated by Mike Keepness.
Includes bibliographical references.

ISBN-13: 978-1-894431-08-8
ISBN-10: 1-894431-08-1

   1. Grey Owl, 1888-1938--Juvenile literature. 2. Conservationists--Canada--Biography--Juvenile literature.
3. Wildlife conservation--Saskatchewan, Northern--Juvenile literature. 4. Saskatchewan, Northern--Biography--Juvenile literature.
5. Authors, Canadian (English)--20th century--Biography--Juvenile literature.
   I. Keepness, Mike, 1981-
   II. Title.

FC541.G75P85 2006   j639.9'092   C2006-901121-4

Printed in Canada
July 2006

Your Nickel's Worth Publishing
Regina, SK.

www.yournickelsworth.com

A Saskatchewan
Product

FOREWORD

Ever since I was a little girl, I've heard stories about the adventures of Grey Owl, my great-great-grandfather, and wished I could have been a part of them. His greatest desire was to protect and preserve Canada's wildlife and vast wilderness.

To everyone reading this book, I hope you enjoy hearing about Grey Owl's life as much as I did. Always remember that people become what they dream.

Tanyann Grey Owl Belaney

"Animals of the forest
are your friends ..."

GREY OWL

PROLOGUE

Grey Owl sat cross-legged on the schoolroom floor and children gathered around as they would for a campfire story. Wearing a fringed deerskin jacket, his black hair in trailing braids, he told stories of animals they had only seen in picture books.

He spoke of his friends: the deer, moose, bear, loon, otter and eagle. But one animal in particular held a very special place in Grey Owl's heart ...

My little brothers and sisters, I am Wa-Sha-Quon-Asin, He-Who-Flies-By-Night, Grey Owl. I come in peace. I come to speak to you of the mountains and the great forests and the rocks and the pure waters of our beautiful land, and the men and animals that have lived here for many moons.

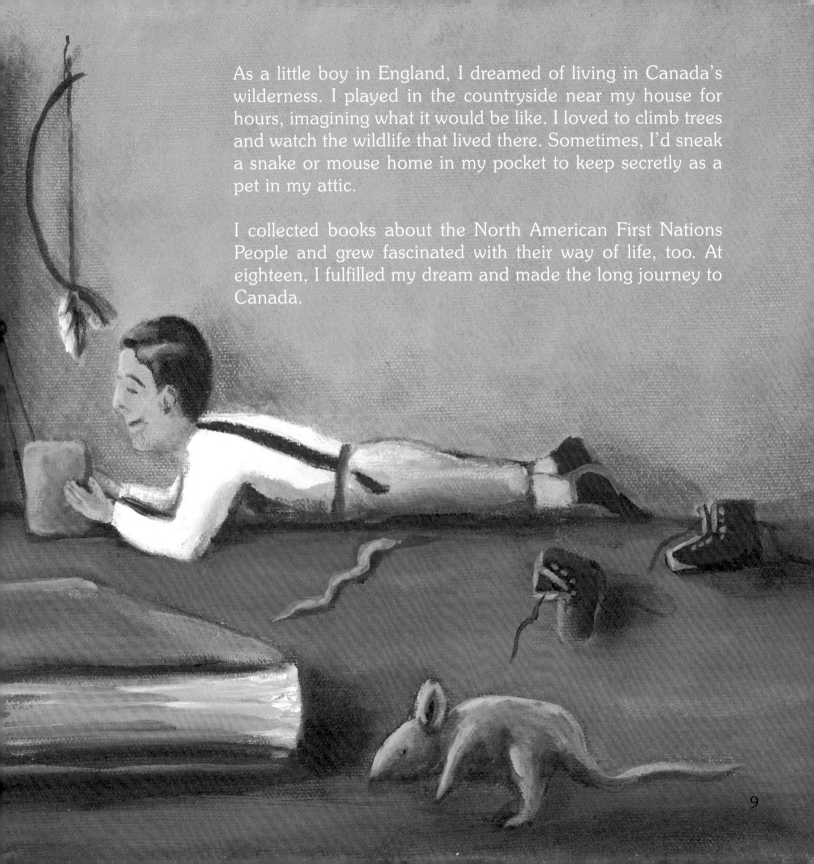

As a little boy in England, I dreamed of living in Canada's wilderness. I played in the countryside near my house for hours, imagining what it would be like. I loved to climb trees and watch the wildlife that lived there. Sometimes, I'd sneak a snake or mouse home in my pocket to keep secretly as a pet in my attic.

I collected books about the North American First Nations People and grew fascinated with their way of life, too. At eighteen, I fulfilled my dream and made the long journey to Canada.

I lived with an Ojibwa family on Bear Island, in the forests of Northern Ontario. They taught me many wonderful traditions. I soon learned how to cook in the wilderness, snowshoe, track different animals and skillfully steer a canoe. I married a beautiful Ojibwa woman who taught me their language. We sat together for hours among walls of green while she braided my hair and helped darken my skin with tree bark.

Her pet owl, which had a wounded wing, befriended me. From his perch high in a tree, his large circular eyes watched our every move. My eagerness to learn and constant curiosity about nature reminded my wife of her pet and she named me Grey Owl.

The more I learned about nature and the magnificent forests, the more I loved it.

I worked for many years as a trapper, forest ranger and hunting guide. As a trapper, I snowshoed many miles into the deep woods, setting my traps for beaver pelts. A few days later, I would go back to check them and hope that I had furs to sell. But before long, too many trappers caused a decline in the beaver population. The beaver was near extinction.

One day when I made the long journey to check my traps, I came across two baby beavers. Their mother had been caught in my trap line and had died. I knew their fur would bring a fine price and I needed the money. But when I looked into their tiny desperate eyes I could not bring myself to sell them.

I named the beavers McGinnis and McGinty and called them the two Macs. To my surprise, I found these creatures to be almost childlike. They whimpered for my affection and hung onto me helplessly with their little hands.

When one of the beaver kits went missing, I searched frantically all day. Then, as the evening sky turned shades of gold, I suddenly heard faint squeals from behind a wall of thick grass. I parted the curtain of grass to take a look and saw the lost beaver kit. To my dismay he was stuck in the middle of a muskeg.

I stepped into the cold wet muck without hesitation, instantly sinking up to my knees. I sank deeper and deeper with each move forward. With one hand, I grabbed hold of a tree branch that extended over the swamp. Waist deep, I was almost there!

I stretched out my arm as far as I could to scoop up the terrified little beaver. I was neck-deep in the cold muskeg before I could safely place him on dry land. Overwhelmed with relief, I decided never to trap beavers again.

I am now the President, Treasurer and sole member of the Society of the Beaver People.

A year later, I decided to give the two Macs a more permanent home. I found a beautiful lake where they could continue to do what beavers do: build beaver lodges and, more importantly, make more beavers.

My heart grew heavy with sadness as we said our goodbyes.
After all, these wonderful creatures had become my children.

Living in the wilderness allowed me to make friends with all kinds of wildlife. One of my best friends was Charlie, a baby moose. He would appear silently out of the forest. The clip-clop of hooves prancing on my wooden porch signaled his presence. Charlie loved to poke his head through the top half of my cabin door, as if to say,

"Hello, Grey Owl, where are the snacks today?"

Charlie's huge shiny wet nose picked up the scent of leftover bannock from my dinner. He would happily sniff and snort until I gave him some. As his velvety-soft mouth gently took the bannock from my hand, I noticed two large bumps growing out of the top of his head.

I told Charlie he would soon have a tough time getting through my doorway!

I adore the Whiskey Jack birds when they come to visit me for food. They land on my finger to squawk, flapping their wings and telling me their daily stories.

Squirrels often scamper up my legs to help themselves to the peanuts stashed in my pockets.

I enjoy all this attention from the forest creatures.

But I missed the companionship of my flat-tailed friends … so I adopted two more beavers. Jelly Roll arrived first, and then Rawhide. Jelly grew to be big and bossy and when Rawhide came along she was very jealous. She constantly picked fights with him.

But one day as I was returning to my cabin, I heard loud grunts and hissing. To my shock and horror, Jelly Roll had been badly hurt and Rawhide was defending her against an enormous male beaver twice his size! The two wrestled viciously and tried to bite each other with their powerful teeth. Rawhide did not back down for an instant. Suddenly the unwanted visitor released his grip and Rawhide chased him away.

I could see that chunks of fur were missing from Rawhide's back as he painfully hobbled back to where Jelly Roll lay. As he snuggled up against her, Jelly Roll made soft noises as if to say, "Thank you." I was very proud of Rawhide. If he had not protected Jelly Roll, she would have been killed. After this, they were the best of friends. Soon they would be the most famous beavers in the world.

Jelly Roll and Rawhide live with me in a beaver paradise on Ajawaan Lake in Prince Albert National Park in northern Saskatchewan. The cabin, named "Beaver Lodge," was built right beside the lake. It has a dirt floor on one side with a hole near the wall so the beavers can swim directly into the lake from inside the cabin.

The first winter they stayed with me, Jelly Roll and Rawhide even built part of their lodge right inside the cabin! Using the front door, they dragged in branches, mud and anything else left lying around. Jelly Roll does not like any mess near her territory, so occasionally I find my scattered papers in her junk pile by the window. I gave up trying to keep a decent broom because they love to carry it around in their mouths.

The legs on my chairs and tables are constantly gnawed down and teeth marks are on every piece of wood in the cabin! I made a special ramp on the side of my canoe so when the beavers are swimming they can climb up into the canoe for a treat of apple slices. Beavers are nocturnal and I have become accustomed to sleeping in the day and writing at my desk during the night.

The Canadian government heard about my conservation work with the beavers and asked if they could make a movie. Film crews were sent out to Beaver Lodge and Jelly Roll and Rawhide became stars! Men, women and children from all over the world have seen the unique and special relationship I have with these "little people."

Grey Owl sat quietly for a moment as he scanned his young audience. The children were spellbound. With a twinkle in his eye and a gentle smile, he reminded them that each animal is special and unique—just as people are—and should be treated with the utmost respect.

"Remember, you belong to Nature, not it to you."

Grey Owl moved toward the schoolhouse doorway to leave but, before disappearing, he turned back. He cupped his hands around his mouth and imitated the sound of a hoot owl.

Grey Owl's call soared through the air as the children waved goodbye.

GLOSSARY

Conservation: Preserving, especially the natural environment.

Extinction: No longer surviving in the world at large or in a specific area.

Muskeg: A swamp or bog in North America, consisting of a mixture of water and partly dead vegetation, often covered by a layer of mosses.

Nocturnal: Active at night.

SOURCES

Belaney, Tanyann Grey Owl, email interview, November 2005.

CBC Film. "Grey Owl" Production, 1972.

Dickson, Lovat. "Wilderness Man," The Strange Story of Grey Owl, 1973.

Geary, John. "Following In Grey Owl's Wake."
http:/www.bearlair.calgreyowl.htm.

Gordon, Irene Ternier, Grey Owl: The Curious Life of Archie Belaney, Altitude Publishing Canada Ltd. 2004.

Grey Owl, The Adventures of Sajo and Her Beaver People. Toronto; Macmillan, 1935.

Grey Owl, The Tree. London, Lovat Dickson Ltd., 1937.

The Canadian Forestry Association. "Grey Owl Biography."
http://collections.ic.gc.ca/canforestry/lowend/greyowl/

The Times. "A Visit with Grey Owl."
http://www.waldervilletimes.com/greyowl.htm